LION, GNAT

Lee Slonimsky

SPUYTEN DUYVIL
New York City

©2017 Lee Slonimsky
ISBN 978-1-944682-68-2

Library of Congress Cataloging-in-Publication Data

Names: Slonimsky, Lee, author.
Title: Lion, gnat / Lee Slonimsky.
Description: New York City : Spuyten Duyvil, [2017]
Identifiers: LCCN 2017028337 | ISBN 9781944682682 (softcover)
Classification: LCC PS3619.L67 A6 2017 | DDC 811/.6--dc23
LC record available at https://lccn.loc.gov/2017028337

For Elizabeth J. Coleman,
Poet Extraordinaire And Extraordinary Friend

Contents

Preface by Elizabeth J. Coleman   xi

Author's Preface

"The Math in a Flower: Walking in Woodstock"	xv
"Flower"	xvii
"Chicory, Mathematician"	xviii

Part One: Electrons Love To Dance

"Lion, Gnat"	3
"Molecules"	4
"Limitations"	5
"Electrons Love to Dance"	6
"Meditation with Wind"	7
"The Humble"	8
"Certain Things Last"	9
"Geometry in Paradise"	10
"Languor"	11
"Bark Birth"	12
"Choir"	13
"Ancestor"	14
"The Noble Savage"	16
"Veins"	18
"Bird Call"	19
"What Nature Meant"	20
"Choir"	21
"Sitting in My Car"	22

Part Two: Near The Johnson Oak

"Winter"	25
"Mice by the Pond"	26
"I am I"	27
"February's Softening Stream"	28
"Change"	29
"Walking"	30
"Talons"	31
"Frog in the Car"	32
"Three Hundred Millionth Birthday"	34
"Near the Johnson Oak"	35
"Dates"	36
"The Counterfeiter"	37
"Weldon Kees"	38
"Those Poems"	39

Part Three: Sorrento, Looking Back

"That Kiss"	43
"Yes or No"	44
"News"	45
"Sorrento, Looking Back"	46
"Flash and Glow"	47
"The Balcony"	48
"Vacation(s)"	49
"The Ambivalence of Love"	50
"Hope"	51
"The South of Spain"	52
"Longing"	53

Part Four: Listen Hard

"Pythagoras Finds Clarity"	57
"Pythagoras Puzzles Over Golden Wings"	58
"Pythagoras's Psyche"	59
"Black Ants, Leaf, Grass"	60
"Listen Hard"	61
"Pythagoras Adjusts to Exile"	62
"Pythagoras: Arrested in Exile"	63
"The Frustrations of Aging"	64
"Xanthes Revenge"	65
"Pythagoras and the Wealthy Stoic"	66
"Transmigration; In the Future"	67

Preface By Elizabeth J. Coleman

In the brief span of our lives, we have the chance to come across a few people who touch our own in a profound way through their work and their friendship. In my life, poet Lee Slonimsky is one of those people. I met him twelve years ago when he was my first poetry teacher at the Westside Y Writers Voice in a class entitled, "Walking with the Sonnet." Lee Slonimsky encouraged me before I earned his encouragement, and, in doing so, changed the course of my life.

Since that time our collaboration has deepened profoundly. Perhaps most significantly for me, I had the great pleasure of translating Slonimsky's sonnet collection, *Pythagoras in Love,* into French (*Pythagoras in Love, Pythagore, Amoureux*, Folded Word Press, 2015). What began as an act of gratitude became an intellectual adventure as Lee Slonimsky and I collaborated on this bilingual collection over the course of a year. It thrilled me that this imaginative and original sonnet sequence, written in the voice of Pythagoras, should have a life in another language, so that it could be read by many more people all over the world.

Slonimsky's unique vision shines through again in *Lion, Gnat*. This is a man of passionate beliefs and intellectual pursuits: his interest in and knowledge of math, his love of nature (he walks in the woods every day and writes as he walks) and of animals; his interest in time and the transmigration of souls; his identification with Pythagoras. Some say there is nothing new under the sun. But there's plenty new in Lee Slonimsky's vision. One of the joys of *Lion, Gnat* is to be reunited with his astonishing world view and his alter ego Pythagoras.

In *Lion, Gnat*, Slonimsky's relationship to time, both human and geological, becomes a more central theme than in his earlier work, as do the complexity of the universe and time's relationship to that complexity.

For example, one of the sonnets in the collection spans 30 million years in evoking the evolution of the whale, and a number of the poems are about our brief chance for human love in the short span of our lives. As Slonimsky writes in the first two lines of his title poem, the first in the collection,

> Complexity determines everything,
> And is the universe's one true love.

He continues in these fourteen lines to describe the evolution of the whale over thirty million years:

> come back in thirty million years and find
> two dozen species, wide variety
> of fin and jaw, of size, for sure of mind;
> while glossy fin is supple, arm is wing,
> blue feathered now, aloft. (The sky its sea.)

Another poem in the collection called "Three Hundred Millionth Birthday" is written in the voice of a fern.

Over and over we see that this is a book about love in nature and lust for nature, interspersed with poems about love between people, always coming back to that deeper love, or lust:

> the lust of molecules to rearrange
> themselves quite differently: as lion, gnat.
> As white dwarf star, as rushing stream; as Alps.
> As backyard in East Acton: swallow's loops.

Just as Slonimsky anthropomorphizes molecules, he does the same with electrons.

Electrons love to dance
while orbiting; romance
their protons while they whirl.
   ("Electrons Love to Dance")

One of the pleasures of Slonimsky's poetry are the moments when he connects the almost infinite with the immediate and personal. In "Flash and Glow, the poem ends,

…the hotel hammock sways, as if the earth
has a vast distant pulse: some fragrant warmth.

And the reader is reminded in reading Slonimsky's Pythagoras poems in this collection why Pythagoras is his alter-ego: Slonimsky gives Pythagoras his own wonder. He writes of Pythagoras's observation of dragonflies ("Pythagoras Puzzles Over Golden Wings")

He's fascinated by their zigzags, whir
Of yellow shimmer-wings, deep love of light;

Obsesses daily over how they fly,
their mapfulness, the vigor, ancient why.
Hypotheses based on wander, flit.

What a delight for a few minutes to share with Slonimsky his interests, and his connection to someone who lived 2,600 years ago. And to experience all this in the context of Slonimsky's skillful sonnets, another passion of the poet's. Tying all his work together is Slonimsky's acute observation of math in nature. In "Chicory, Mathematician," he writes,

The petals range in number, narrowly:
Thirteen to nineteen, composite or prime.

In the end, Slonimsky's poems are about connection: among epochs, among people, among sentient beings, and among all living things. As the poet puts it in another Pythagoras poem, ("Black Ants, Leaf, Grass"):

He formed a rough belief
in common origin: ants. Lion. Grass.

And that leads us to transmigration, another belief of Pythagoras/Slonimsky, the ultimate "connection." E.M. Forster admonishes, "Only connect." That is the essence of being human. Lee Slonimsky gives us the gift of connecting in ways we did not know were possible.

Author's Preface

The Math In A Flower:
Walking In Woodstock

For over a decade, I have been writing most of my poems on walks. They generally tend to be short poems, often sonnets, given the limitations of time this method imposes. I write on folded squares of blank paper that I carry in my pockets, pausing briefly each time I need to write a line down, and subsequently pausing again to reread and revise. Later, at home or my office, I type the poem on a computer and make further revisions.

I mostly write nature poetry, so the locale for my "poetry walks" is of crucial significance. I view the locale where I walk as a kind of collaborator with me on these poems, it often providing an inspiration or catalyst in the form of some aspect of nature that gives me an image or an idea. My poetry walk nowadays is often one through the outskirts of Woodstock, along Lower and Upper Byrdcliffe Roads and Glascoe Turnpike.

A recent experience in which my walk seemed to co-author a poem involved the beautiful blue flower, chicory. I do not have even the lay person's knowledge of flowers (that I may have of birds and trees), and I had not noticed this flower, which is common along a section of Lower Byrdcliffe Road, previously. One day, fascinated as ever by the role that math plays in nature, I happened to pause before one, stoop, and count how many petals it had. Nineteen. Wondering what the genetic history might have been that led to this particular number, I went on to count several others. Fourteen. Seventeen. Fifteen. There was no exact replication of number from one to the next, rather a range from the low to high teens. I puzzled over it. Barring accident or disease, humans go through life with two arms and two legs, not a combination that might add up to five in this person, three in the next, etc. So I wondered about a genetic narrative that provided only a range for petals. This was obviously not the sophisticated questioning of an evolutionary biologist, and maybe petals shouldn't really be compared to limbs, but I'm a poet, not a scientist. And my bafflement inspired two poems.

Before concluding with the poems, I should mention one or two additional catalysts for them. Beyond observation of nature I am (as mentioned above) concerned with the role that math plays in nature, and toward that end have chosen a poetic and historical alter ego for myself, the Greek philosopher Pythagoras. I've published two collections from Pythagoras's imagined point of view, *Pythagoras in Love* and *Logician of the Wind,* (the former translated into French by the brilliant poet Elizabeth J. Coleman), and have continued to write and publish poems from Pythagoras's point of view. That's how I came in the first poem to transform my experience with the chicory into a dilemma that might have startled Pythagoras two thousand, five hundred years ago. I fictionalized my observation for this poem, because the poem grew too complicated and unwieldy otherwise. The second poem, a triolet, was truthful to my observation but did not involve Pythagoras.

Flower

These thin blue petals crowd together so,
it's hard to count them. But Pythagoras
can gently bend their heads into sunlight
and patiently observe until he knows
there are nineteen. He's pleased with his eyesight,
a mild west breeze, a gleaming abacus,
the virtues of pure math. But wait: *nineteen*,
he thinks, seems awfully random. Odd. And prime.

He counts four more blue flowers, all the same;
the breeze picks up; a broken branch sags...moans,
as if in sympathy with his distress
at nature's strangeness. Quite the mystery,
where *nineteen* came from, so haphazardly
that life itself could be all chance. Unless...

Thoughts drift off slowly. Black clouds in the west.
A flock of thirteen birds. Lightning. *No rest.*

Chicory, Mathematician

The petals range in number, narrowly:
thirteen to nineteen, composite or prime.

This flower loves math more than you or me!

The petals range in number, narrowly,
aimed at a pleasant blue geometry.

She loves to *count*, like timber wolves to roam.

The petals range in number, narrowly:
thirteen to nineteen, composite or prime.

Lion, Gnat

PART ONE:

ELECTRONS LOVE TO DANCE

Lion, Gnat

Complexity determines everything,
and is the universe's one true love.

The first four-legged whale is primitive:
come back in thirty million years and find
two dozen species, wide variety
of fin and jaw, of size, for sure of mind;
while glossy fin is supple arm is wing,
blue-feathered now, aloft. (The sky its sea.)

Complexity's the language of pure change;
the lust of molecules to rearrange
themselves quite differently: as lion, gnat.
As white dwarf star, as rushing stream; as Alps.
As backyard in East Acton: swallow's loops.

Flux is the core of steel no matter what.

Molecules

When billions link they *texture* into forms
as various as steel, or swarms of bees;
as streamsmoothed stones, slow snow, green windchopped seas;
sand grains, blue jays.

                        The brilliant sun that warms
this chilly forest on the brink of spring
itself is hydrogen by trillions cubed
and I myself am merely matter moving.

(A soul's existence never has been proved.)

Yet beauty may not be mechanical
alone, or inspiration a machine.
If genius were a matter just of will,
it should be rampant, but it's rarely seen.

This late June leaf, though green, drifts slowly down
and lands without the faintest hint of sound,
as if it's only image, or pure thought;
display by breeze and light of startling wit.

Limitations

I'd like to have an hour
inside a molecule
to get a sense, the flavor
of how its inner rule
over atoms held in bondage—
the core design of matter—
feels to those experiencing
autocracy of charge.

Electrons in their orbits,
their never ending spin:
what the view might be from there
where nature truly begins.

As it is I am resigned
to textbooks and their diagrams,
heaps of scholarly papers.

A half drained cup of coffee,

sunlight gleaming on
this aquamarine paperweight,

ruling my square desk.

Electrons Love To Dance

while orbiting; romance
their protons while they whirl.

There's no solidity
to rock or diamond, pearl,

since atoms' empty space
is empty as
anti-matter's swirl.

Meditation With Wind

I love to get in touch with what's inside:
my *atomscape*, yes largely empty space
but also whirs and flashes. Nuclei;
the grammar of small molecules; no trace
of what we know as flesh. Just atoms' spin,
taut miniatures from stars' hot origins.

Perhaps it's odd to meditate this way,
relax amidst primordial dazzle-essence,
too tiny for our eyes by far. To stay
back in Big Bang, the first grand luminescence,
that bubbled into matter.

                                            But I'm fine
with sleeping so with atoms, now and then,
reminders of another world. The wind
agrees by rustling branches. Once. Again.

The Humble

"I am *not* nobody, and I am trying."

However modest ants may look
to us
each one is President
of his or her own life.
No Congress or Supreme Court
to wrestle with,
just an inner voice
saying "drop the pebble;
it's a thousand times your weight,"
another saying "let's plod onward,
home's around that tree root
gleaming black in morning rain,
and only gutless ants
do not find the verve."

President of perfect beauty,
glistening ant body
five hundred million years
in the making.
Quivering antennae
in love with light and shadow.

Certain Things Last

The scent of lemon trees far out at sea
without cargo, or even wind, to explain:
you smelled it too. I saw your puzzlement;

we shrugged away confusion, sipped our jasmine tea
and watched seasparkle from our deck chairs, then
reflected on what such little miracles meant.

"Perhaps ten million years ago
this was the sunwashed valley; groves of trees
so thick their scent persists," I said. You laughed:

"Some things just can't be explained."

                                            A breeze
picked up, and lemons vanished. Sea turned rough,
our chairs began to slide, then we got up,
observing quite a leap from a blue fish
that surged skyward, then dove in a gleaming loop.
I took your hand; we balanced; air was chill.

And soon the sun returned, and sea was still.

Geometry In Paradise

The falling tree was caught so perfectly
by a neighbor's branch: to teach geometry
of triangles to nearby woods, and birds.
No teacher could explain as well—in words—
as this late March collegiality
among sky-spearing pines;

                                    no diagrams
by Euclid have the impact of the *wild*
obeying angle-law; (trees do their sums
as well as the most math-precocious child),

and birds exceed tree math in spirals, swerves,
inventiveness with vectors and swift curves.
The sun's a scholar of high-angled rays,
while math's in use each time a gnarled branch sways;
math's everywhere: in synapses, veinlets, leaf-nerves.

Languor

As I fade away,
I look in the spaces between the trees

for green atoms bouncing back and forth,
trunk to trunk,
green atoms I might hitch a ride on but

their trail is too flimsy and mild
and I would drop straight through them,
thud against October leaves
and chill in sodden soil.

Bark Birth

The longest novel ever written is
the evolution of the modern tree:
the chapter on barkbirth especially,
which teeth midwifed

(*teeth's threat* which led to us
as well: to skulls then brains).

                        Our wordrich phase
of evolution has you out, midday
with pen and pad, to see what trees might say
in one footnote;

                September sun, leaflaze
evoking all the early memories
of swamps, first dinosaurs, enormous ferns:
companions in explosive growth of green.

Trees nod their crowns in soft late summer breeze,
as vastness of one sentence slows your pen:

a fumbled start, cross off, begin again.

Choir

Crafty at her craft,
this ancient oak winds gaunt and well-knobbed branches
around still other gnarled and sprawling limbs
to be the *Queen of Writhe*.

Birds that flit within the coils chirp on,
symphony of jumble,
choir of zig and zag.

Ancestor

"There was a light film of dust, such as accumulates in
the cleanest room when it is left shut up."
    Raymond Chandler, *The Lady in the Lake*

Dust is at the very core of the universe.
Stars formed from clouds of dust.
So did we.

So when you're sitting at your baby grand,
11 AM on a Tuesday morning,
sunlight from the bay window
luminescing its polished ebony,
and you're troubled by a few spinning motes
or a smatter of speckles on one onyx key,
say hello to your venerable,
cosmic, distinguished and meek ancestor,
a speck of *Is*
that wouldn't harm a fly.

The meek not only inherit the earth,
they *are* the earth.

And when your gaze strays to
the glimmering ocean beyond the window,
breezetossed winks of seaspray
blinking back at you in agreement
that you're both a matter of dust
arranged, rearranged by the cosmos
in *Is*'s eternal howl;
your first tentative keystrike in "C"
puts an exclamation
on slim aeronautics of dust,

and your second seems to rejoice
at how smoothly one intrepid note
comes in for a filmy landing
on a stretch of mahogany
as blank as primordial zero.

The Noble Savage

You can feel 5:00's thunderstorm
in this morning's haze:
haze frail enough to poke a stick through
if the sky were your tent.

Weather is wandering
from bronze-of-late-summer
to fall,
and that's your sole amibition:
to wander right along with it,
leaving your 9 to 5 prison behind,
just as this cold breeze flees
the yellow seethe of July.

Green & York is open this morning—
stockbrokers to the exceptionally wealthy—
but your own gray desk is vacant,
lathered in harbor, mist-shrouded light,
but no activity there beyond
the photons that also fill
these sparse pine woods
where you stroll midmorning,
breathing deep your new and cone-tanged freedom.

The way dust motes spin in shafts of light,
perhaps concealing a few flying seeds,
reminds you of newfound obscurity:

only these trees for clients,
only the angles of sunlight and breeze
for profits and losses,
only the sky for a boss.

When the thunderstorm turns up early—
fat raindrops, black sky,
with goldening cracks of quickbolt
just before noon—
you're inclined to give storm its freedom too,
this wandering, electric savage,
just as noble as you are.

Veins

The branches culminate in fluffed out twigs
resembling capillaries. Leaves have veins.
The trunk's a body, roots a swarm of legs,
and branches culminate in fluffed out twigs.
These are our ancestors. Awareness sings!
No overestimating what this means.
The branches culminate in fluffed out twigs
resembling capillaries. Leaves have veins.

Bird Call

"Prettee—pretteee—pretteeee."

I cannot agree.
Yes the firs are sleek
slender spires of green
that calm a clouding sky,
but oh the smudges on the snow.
Foul streaks and smears from cars that go
along the state road half a mile away.

I'd like to live here, but only in the past,
when snow alone fell through the windy air
and shadows came from light and not exhaust.
How glorious this frozen stream was then:
when after clouds parted
the red and gold of sunset shimmered like
the seal upon a world encased in ice,
a mirror for the stars about to come
and midnight's sliver moon: pearl scimitar.

What Nature Meant

"Thoreau sat here," an ink-scrawled stump informs,
midmorning's sunsplash brightening these words
that speak of anti-bustle, *ponder*, birds,
and Massachusetts: mostly woods and farms.

He was your inspiration long ago,
and why not sit here, too? The air is sweet,
"drones run amuck" a fairly distant threat;
the loudest sounds nearby a bullfrog's, crow's.

You sit, and up above, spy slightest break
in tangled canopy of dense June leaves.
Beyond, pure blue where nothing modern moves;
no smoke nor smudges, glazed exhaust. You ache
for endless skies without a scar or taint,
the kind Thoreau saw then. What nature meant.

Sitting In My Car

How many billions of years
forged these veins
that pulse in my fingertips
as I scribble these lines?

I can see eons echo
in the drooping branchery
of a beech tree dangling
against a window,
lightly brushed by sunlight.

Tree, my distant relative,
green-cored essence of complexity
as tangled as my veins.

Tree itself a late arrival
in a saga of billions of years.

Tree that would loan me a vein
if I needed to borrow one.

I'm reluctant to start the car's engine,
a rumbling axe that will split the air.

Part Two:

Near The Johnson Oak

Winter

Intense absence
of any guiding hand:

just this clearing in the woods,
sunlit.

The trickle of a stream
in the distance,
a black cold narrative
in a world where snow
knows no boundaries,

and nothing's brighter than
blue air.

MICE BY THE POND

This winter's late, then hesitates, but ice
cannot resist and subtly starts to form,
and soon enough props up pond-crossing mice.
This winter's late, then hesitates, but ice:

the hawks find mice no matter how they race,
and keep such *ease-of-prey* until it's warm.
This winter's late, then hesitates, but ice
cannot resist and subtly starts to form.

"I Am I"

Such an austere stare, this oak tree has;
staring down late autumn wind
as if it has no fear.

And then it's April and its trunk has bent
a quarter of the way due east,
so fierce was that late
January gale,

and still it stares you down now.

Nothing worth fearing
for it
from a deep woods stroller like yourself,
or crawling ant; or perching hawk
or breezes riffling
brand new leaves,
leaves that are its green and countless pride.

"I am I" its slow look says;
its silent, slow voice roars.

"No winter ever brings me down."

February's Softening Stream,

ice-shedding in this land
of ever-warming winters,
sounds at first like muted wind
heard through bramble, branches.

We're approaching in the densest woods
in dimming sunlight,
the color of a particularly pale
Valentine's Day.

But there's no wind:
only speeding water
breaking up ice,

a February ghost
of Aprils past.

Change

I open my coat
and spring arrives. Warm wet wind,
blowing like it's June

Walking

The snow slows me up,

walking.

The temptation is
to blend into the air,
the same way flakes merge
with snow already on the ground.

The slower I walk,
the more I merge.

Sunlight, for a moment:
snowflakes dazzle.

I twist around to look at them
from right inside the snow,
and now they seem to follow me
everywhere I go.

Talons

Voluptuous midmorning for the wrens!
With insects flitting thickly through moist air,
abundance is a feast. Wrens are asleep by noon,
leaf-shielded from the sun;
the storm that hurried the bugs still miles away.

And we look out our windows, gorged as well
on sleeping-late slow love in lovely woods,
well-cottaged in the dark green wilderness.

As wrens eat gnats so hawks take wrens:
asleep, awake. The storm begins to ripple leaves.

One plummet's sudden, silent. Splatter! Rise
with taloned, broken prey. The first fat drops descend,
like silver, solder drops; shimmering.

We're cozy on the bedside. Bloody woods

shiver.

Frog In The Car

Tiny yes, a tadpole no.
He'll never be a bullfrog.

Stalking the windshield
for an exit.

Offspring of evolutionary chance,
just like you.

Doesn't grasp the concept of glass.
When he rests you can see his pulse,
his tiny glossy body trembling
with seeming fragility,
but he's been here three
hundred million years
so you know he must be tough
in a way.

How he got here
you don't know
(on the dashboard or on planet earth)
but you feel you have to *stop*
and let him out
before his nerves
are mush.

Window down now,
a newspaper shuttle
will be his rescuer,
but then he leaps without an aid:
and glides a breeze to safety.

The vast blue sky's awash in hope
for freedom everywhere!

Car picks up speed and forest blurs
to his perfect pitch of emerald green.

Three Hundred Millionth Birthday

The breezes swish my fellow ferns, but I
am motionless, so deep in thought. The lie
that deep time tells is this: "all green, the same"
but I was here so long before the grass
that I was ancient when grass made its name
for sleekness, shimmer, meadow-silk. The past
is *princed* by me, pure royalty. I rule
all others in my modesty. I'll rule a while,
but let me not be so competitive.

We are all children of the sun.

Near The Johnson Oak

A scimitar, a vase, a sphere: the moon
can be all these, and more. Midnight, dim day.

You walk in wind where gaunt oak branches moan
and last leaves flutter: *this*, your usual way,
seems somehow ghostly at twilight.

                                                  Moonstrange,
gust-cleaved, as if much time has passed—
your name has changed—you've reached some awesome age
and yet, you know the path. Each tree. Each twist
in moonsplashed shadow-trail.

                                          You pass a youth—
the slightest glance—you realize he is you!
You're tempted to pursue, but fear you both
together: what your meeting up might show
about how slippery reality
can be in moon's slow light. Halved by one tree.

Dates

It's 1482
and that sounds old

now

but then it was the present.

The prow of time's boat
cutting through
blue green, limpid waters.

Our time will be drowned
like that one was.

And soon.

No theory of physics will rescue us.
It's 2395?

2017 will have been just the sparkle of sunlight
on a broken window pane
in the country house we used to own
somewhere near Never.

And that's ok.
2702 is on the way.

And it won't be real either,
just the dream of our lonely Orb
spinning somewhere in space.

The Counterfeiter

In 1438, a sunny day
and rain the night before have left a gleam,
a path well-puddled. On his wary way
to transfer silver coins, John hears a scream
a ways off to his left, through thickest woods.

Instinctively he clutches his wealth close;
discerns the clank of armor. And he broods
about a swung-high axe: King's troops are fierce.
They may have caught a thief just now;

                                               listen:

but there's no sound of gallop, splashing trot,
just furtive birds who chirp and softly whistle.
Distracted, John trips on a twisted root:
yet fear finds peace in his quick sudden sprawl.

Blue sky—still free!—no harm in just one fall.

Weldon Kees

The boneblue chilliness of these waters—
October wind whipped—silences poems.

Inertia but for the seahawk who roams
higher than clouds. Near sunlight and laughter:
while blue water glimmers.

                                  One broken oak moans,
wind-twisted not far from the shore.
You're caught in between slow skies and disaster.
A letter unopened, a phone call unanswered.
Oblivion's key. The deep windstreaked water.

Those Poems

My cold struggle to write a poem,
this Amherst morning.
Sharply, almost savagely bare trees,
a foot of snow
and silence all around me
as if winter were screaming.

Not far away,
those poems were written.

Metallic gray clouds
reinforce the deadness.
Only when a dash of cardinal color
flares into view
am I reminded
that a whitish—gold sun can turn red
in the coming seethe of seasons.

Poetry stays silent
but a sudden gust of wind
eddies frail flakes of snow
into a fleeting whirl.

Part Three:

Sorrento, Looking Back

That Kiss

Our glasses were drained: late sunlight filled them now,
slow-tinting red, sad dregs of day; the sea
beyond the terrace wind-creased, dark. So slow,
this fading afternoon, we tried to flee
from time itself with talk. We knew things couldn't last
but here the Bay balmed memory, and hope
took flight like gulls, that chased light to the west.
At least when chatter filled our space. The creep
of starry black returned us to our room:
our next day's tickets, jobs, some arguments…
Then suddenly the salt tanged vastness made more sense
than acrimony, bills, contentious home,
and we stepped back outside for one long kiss.
Slow, quiet waves. Boats' gliding lights. Bliss.

Yes Or No

"You're married—really—well so what?
That's travel risk. Though this is Crete, we could
be anywhere: Jamaica, Cannes or Spain.
Sometimes we need to leave our lives behind.

"Not everyone can mate for life like birds. And yes,
oh please, I will go on another week or two.
Your tears are silly. We're just traveling through."

A stucco balcony gleams in the dawn,
sun's yellow glaze on rosedeep pink. Its view:
tiled slanted roofs for several blocks. Then sea,
where diamond breezeless glitter stretches west.

We lounge with juice and coffee, waking up,
and contemplate the narrow hillside lanes
where fuller café breakfasts might be found
in this or that side street dining place.

"You hate your husband? Near enough to kill?
I'll listen but…I'm not a violent man.
Meanwhile a toasted bagel…Swiss cheese…yes?!
Sounds perfect for this windless morning, yes."

News

The knock. On a hotel door.

Telegram.

(In those days people still sent them.)

You stepped out on the balcony:

sun
lathered the Bay of Naples
like light was washing water,
and all the essence of the world
had been made into gleam.

The vista softened news just so,
and it was not (entirely)
unexpected.

You'd never felt so quite alone
but there, over there, some sailboats glided;

salt tang coasted in on a breeze
and this day too would end.

Sorrento, Looking Back

It's funny what associations last,
and bridge the gulf of years. *That lemonade
a vendor used to hawk*, as fragrant as
a sunwashed grove. We passed him daily on our walks:
beyond the road, blue shimmer of the bay.

In bed by noon, the afternoon a swoon
of love, heat-drained fatigue, then rootlessness.
There is no wandering like that of youth.

Awakening at 5 PM, the terrace next—
iced tea with lemon as the sun declined—
the future vague as filmy dusk's descent,
its early stars bejeweling sky and sea.

*Now, hint of lemon on this sudden breeze
from who knows where, quite like a sorcerer:*

*it conjures you from staid old Central Park.
Almost that swoon. Almost that morning walk.*

Flash And Glow

Sorrento of my dreams—

                    I have returned,
alone, years later, on a business trip—

and now it's Sunday and I watch the loops
a white gull flies. No matter how I yearned
to speak, to touch you once: you were like stone.

Long after now, sea soothes, breezes caress;
the sun dips slowly toward the silent west.

All perfect moments are as if on loan,
so fragile, quick. Saved by memory as best we can,
or art, or dream.

                We stayed here but a week,
and what a flash and glow back then. I look
for comfort now at wings, red rays on sand;

the hotel hammock sways, as if the earth
has a vast, distant pulse: some fragrant warmth.

The Balcony

Ghent's never called "the city of lovers";
Ghent's never given its due.

But on one twilight evening with lights in the distance,
a mist knows how to caress us.

Vacation(s)

We're nineteen once, but not again. "Why not?"
you'd asked back then; "let's go by summer sea.
So beautiful, and just five days: let's be
as free as oldtime travel was. We'll sit
on deck and live the breeze." And so we went
to Europe that one time, sunwashed, all new,
with not a clue that we were almost through.

Our squabble came in Belgium, there in Ghent;
hot August day, the central square. And now,

I'm back. The food is great. The cobblestones
in every lane *evoke*, like city bones,
and what perspective thirty years allow.

I wander one dim alley, call your name:
and silence tells me time itself's to blame.

The Ambivalence Of Love

A narrow street in Ghent, Belgium. Dark blue;
late dusk. Lit windows are small golden squares,
and you slouch in an entranceway.

                                    So true,
that this may be the end. And please, no tears.
You hear a rustling, flights above; perhaps
she's coming down now: *this is it!* Beware,
you tell yourself, of being weak; no hopes
remain of reconciling.

                        Stare and stare,
but she's not there. You must have heard a breeze.

So emptiness replaces stress. The sky
goes almost black; more windows come ablaze.
The minutes drag: go up the stairs? You sigh
at fate's perversity—you need your pride—
and leave.

                Night drowns you in its poignant tide.

Hope

The porthole shows us snow at sea, a storm
that wasn't forecast. We are extra warm:
the cabin's heated well. And we're so close
to the elements, our front row seats excite!
We've argued half the voyage, felt quite lost
but here's a different mood, almost delight.

And then a serpent head looms up no more
than fifteen feet away, and ten above
the black, wind-tumulted waves; its red-eyed stare
is not the sort inspiring thoughts of love.
A slender long neck, compact head, two eyes
unhappy and vindictive. We might flee
but options are quite sparse with snow at sea;

we hope the serpent feats we've heard about

are lies.

The South Of Spain

I can't recall the name: a city so strange,
and not on any map. Canals galore,
stone parapets and streets all of great age.
No welcome center; no-one to give a tour.
We kayaked under bridges: water gleamed
as black as if of incredible depth;

occasionally onlookers tossed some flowers our way.

An odd thought occurred to us:
here, no death
or, at least, not much,
with nothing else exactly as it seemed,
but where this city was, we couldn't say.

Our boat would glide exquisitely
as if its polished wood were made of air,
skimming the black – just so delicately –
yet never did we seem to get anywhere.

Except:

in love we stayed.

Perhaps we left by dream as we'd arrived,
and look back with a fondness
sublime as late day sky.

Longing

This blue hotel is long in disrepair;
the lake gleams good as new however, *now*.
Blue paint has whitened under summer's sear.
This blue hotel is long in disrepair;
these empty windows cannot shed a tear.
And winter's only resident's a crow.
This blue hotel is long in disrepair;
the lake gleams good as new however, *now*.

Part Four:

Listen Hard

Pythagoras Finds Clarity

    after Shakespeare's no. 60

The way these waves break on the pebbled shore
shows how profoundly nature's ruled by math;
advance, retreat, like the ocean is at war
with its own tidal impulse. A clear path
to understanding lies right here, he thinks,
to comprehensive laws and theorems, truth.
How foam seduces, morning sunlight winks
at steady intervals;

                      numbers reveal
the deepest structure of the universe.
More evidence in how gulls coast, then wheel
and dive for fish, their competition fierce,
reminding him of scholars arguing:

maneuvers math-made at their primal source;

what understanding watching waves can bring.

Pythagoras Puzzles Over Golden Wings

(After "Pieces del Sol" by Katherine Hastings)

Their pace of flutter has some formula,
including sunlight's angles, fear of shade,
whatever math they're born with, learn from wind.

He's fascinated by their zigzags, whir
of yellow shimmer-wings, deep love of light;

obsesses daily over how they fly,
their mapfulness, the vigor, ancient why.
Hypothesizes based on wander, flit.

But no math intervenes or clarifies,
and one day sudden winds disturb them all:
concealment in the weeds; airborne, a sudden stall,
or dive. Their skills more random, he decides
than first impression hints. They're like sunlight,
in fragments that can fly. Adroit and bright.

Pythagoras's Psyche

Luxuriance is beautiful: the green
and wild entanglement of woods;
minutae of their flowers. How birds preen
their feathers in bright sun. Glossily. These roads,
when wagon dust clears, sparkle too with light;
two pine trees lean together, are in love.

But for all May's charisma, it's not right
to find allure in chaos. Hawk, above,
is perfect in ellipses. And the sun
won't vary in its arc across the sky.

Yet solace in perfection fades so soon,
while jumble fascinates. He wonders why.

Two voices deep within him, maybe three:
and often they profoundly disagree.

Black Ants, Leaf, Grass

It wasn't easy in the ancient world
to understand the bond between a tree
and animals, and all humanity:
one common origin. Vast time had toiled
near-endlessly to make deep differences
among a rosebush, chipmunk, lion, ant;
and as for trees, never a modest hint
of kinship with the walking. Or a sense
of common parents, but Pythagoras
went walking in cool woods, and a round leaf
fell on his hand, and he perceived a vein
in its smooth texture. Just about the same
as on his hand. He formed a rough belief
in common origin: ants. Lion. Grass.

Listen Hard

A lilting, *prettee* note with swallow tails
of sound that flits from branch to branch. Five times,
repeated as a chorus; and they rhyme
with hammering of a woodpecker:
                                            sound swells
with chirps and caws, and plaintive coos, until
cacophony blurs numbers under sound
and substitutes an April din that fools
a listener with anarchy. Astounds
Pythagoras, who knows that harmony
is all math-based and rhythmic, like the sky
at purple twilight. Or the waves that roll
on endless sunwashed shores. "*Prettee; prettee*"
reminds him of the principles of Pi,
hypotenuse, square root. Math makes him whole.

Pythagoras Adjusts To Exile

How slowly sunlight fills the east at first;
a cloud-cloaked sunrise *essencing* a pause:
big silence, long drawn breath, reflection's laws
away from hurry (civilization's curse).

Out here, a level plain, a neutral space;
his only colleagues wind and soaring birds,
where he can *feel* existence without words,
and read light's language, skyfill's slow-wrought pace.

Well far away, due south, the day begins:
carts rolling over paving stones, the smell
of foodstuffs, livestock; cries of vendors, smoke
from newly lit house fires.

      His big mistake:
to live long in that world and lose his soul.

The wind picks up. A slanted elm tree moans.

Pythagoras: Arrested In Exile

His prisoner's assignment: count the trees
on ninety wooded *hektos*, property
of Metapontum royalty He sees
no way to find a formula for sprawl;
and tangle – mayhem – wind-cleaved branchery
(last night's storm's wild and murderous assault),
do not allow for trigonometry
or other measures.

                    Now late afternoon,
he's spent, his only thought a cooling breeze,
a rippling stream. He naps but must awaken soon:
if spotted by a guard he could return
to underground entombment, endless dark
where madness lurks, and awful silence burns
a hole in any thought. He struggles awake:
discovery would be his fatal mistake.

The Frustrations Of Aging

It's hard to gauge the speed of falcon flight,
when birds come hurtling toward you from a cloud;
the calculation strains the best eyesight.

It's hard to gauge the speed of falcon flight
at noon, sunset, or late one starry night;

Pythagoras can't manage. Now he'll brood.

It's hard to gauge the speed of falcon flight,
when birds come hurtling toward you from a cloud.

Xanthes' Revenge

The bath's been scooped from softest shale, but still
the labor took two years. Xanthes' wealth
allows for breathless whims. The hillside pool,
bejeweled, spring fed, breathtaking sunribbed view
of Athens' west; has slowly helped his health.
He bathes in shimmer; morning makes life new,
and though his walk has slowed, his back has bent,
he can't recall when sapphire water's meant
so much. *Rejuvenation.* For a while.

He lost his only son in that fool's war,
but helped finance revenge: conspiracy.
The gleaming knife, aloft for all to see
in Speaker's Square; a fierce descent that tore
the tyrant's life from flesh and made it ghoul.

And *still*, that aching sadness, in this pool;
but yet sunlight and water are like balm.
Below, the city dazzles. Makes him calm.

Pythagoras And The Wealthy Stoic

He's eyed the house for years, since it was built
on terraced precipice, half mountain high,
the steepest slope. Each terrace with a pool.

This morning, walking, sunlight in his eyes:
he knows the hike up there will take a while,
but the time has come. As if he's called to it;
the whole house shimmers as though made of jewels.

Inside, he hears, asceticism rules

despite the owner's wealth.

                                      (Philosopher himself),
let the two of them converse, no matter what
their past has been. He is a stoic too, of sorts,
for it's just wind and trees that life's about:
their math. Their youthful clash was over *her*,
so long ago. Now they'll discuss more abstract truth.

Transmigration; In The Future

His final lecture of the day is done,
perspectives on pure trigonometry;
his "teaching aids" distinctive branches. When
the sun goes low all angles blur; truths flee
the classroom for deep shadows.

                                                He finds rest
on one gnarled branch, and settles his blue wings;
observes his youthful pupils flying loops
above tall trees. Sometimes he might insist
on their retracing angles learned in class,
but not today: his favorite pupil sings
while others freelance flight. He has great hopes
for four or five; they're agile, oh so fast.

When human he'd loved teaching, mentoring,
and that's unchanged. He's richer than a king.

Acknowledgements

I would like to express my deep gratitude to the editors of the following journals in which some of the poems in *Lion, Gnat* first appeared, sometimes in different form: "Lion, Gnat," *Angle* (UK), Issue 8, 2016; "Talons," *Blueline*, No. XXXVIII (38), 2017; "The Noble Savage," *Green Hills Literary Lantern* XXVI, 2015; "Geometry in Paradise," *The Homestead Review*, No. 35, Spring 2016; "Ancestor," *The Homestead Review* No. 36, Fall 2015; "Frog in the Car," *Millers Pond Poetry Magazine*, Winter 2017; "Winter," *Muddy River Poetry Review*, Spring 2017; "The Math in a Flower: Walking in Woodstock," Will Nixon's blog, willnixon.com, October 23, 2015; "Flash and Glow," *Per Contra*, Issue 40, Summer 2016; "The Ambivalence of Love" and "Listen Hard," *Trinacria*, Issue No. 15, Spring 2016; and "What Nature Meant," *Trinacria*, Issue No. 16, Fall 2016.

Tod Thilleman, Editor and Publisher of Spuyten Duyvil Press, has been steadfast and amazing in his support for my work. So has Elizabeth J. Coleman been in her support, and Elizabeth's editorial contribution to *Lion Gnat,* the manuscript of which she has read and commented on extensively, has been brilliant and invaluable. I am also forever indebted to cover comment writers Tim Suermondt, Barbara Ungar, and Pui Ying Wong, all extraordinary poets themselves. Hammett Award winning novelist Carol Goodman, my gifted and beautiful wife, and my brilliant daughter Dr. Nora Slonimsky, recent CUNY Ph.D., have given painstaking "rankings" over the years which were crucial in compiling this ms. Last but not least, I have been encouraged (and educated) over nearly 50 years of writing poetry by many people, and I can only name a few here (twenty, to pick a round number), with profuse apologies to many others who should be listed: Joe Benevento, Stu Bartow, Peter Bricklebank, Sharon Israel (Cucinotta), Rosemary Donnelly, Sandy Eastoak, Jack Foley, Rachel Hadas, Katherine Hastings, Miriam Kotzin, the late Dr. Daniel Hoffman, X. J. "Joe" Kennedy, Roger Lathbury, Harry Steven Lazerus, Howard Levine, Al Lewis, Mike Robbins, Joe Salemi, A. E. Stallings, and Ginger F. Zaimis.

LEE SLONIMSKY has published eight books of poetry, a chapbook, and a collaborative chapbook with Katherine Hastings. Partnering with his wife, Hammett Prize winning novelist Carol Goodman, he has co-written the Black Swan Rising trilogy of urban fantasy novels, and he has also written a hedge fund mystery novel under his own name, *Bermuda Gold*. Finally, reflecting both his own deep love of animals and his interest in the vegetarian historical figure Pythagoras, he has recently started a humane investing "side pocket" to his hedge fund Ocean Partners LP, which is called Green Hills Partners LP.